VISIONS OF A MADMAN

by

pgh

Dedicated to my
Mom (1911-2000) and
Dad (1908-2002)

VISIONS OF A MADMAN

INTRODUCTION

A glimpse into the schizophrenic mind
(Originally published in 1972
with revisions since then by the author)

pgh, now 74, was once compared to Ken Kesey and Kurt Vonnegut in a college textbook on Abnormal Psychology (1972) as having similar but false views of insanity and the insane with his poem, SELF-KNOWLEDGE.

He continues to struggle with reality but has been married for over 23 years and has been taking care of their 11 year old Maine Coon, who he named MaiLuv (MyLove), who kept his mind off suffering with cluster migraines for 6 of those 10 years until he found his own solution (edible THC) to them after a 12 year stint of trying numerous prescribed treatments which just made his condition worse ending up with Methadone for daily use and Percocet for extreme pain.

One of the drugs prescribed early on was OxyContin which doctors now consider practically immoral.

Though he has been free of cluster migraines for over 6 years, he battles occasional migraines which his solution for the cluster migraines has proved ineffectual and actually worsens his condition.

Though most days his pain is only between 1-3 on a scale of 10 being the worse, occasionally the pain reaches 8-10 for which he has to get a shot of Toradol but now that too has become ineffectual and he relies on Imitrex (Sumatriptan) pills to get him through his life, about 1 every 3 days during attacks.

When he was only 9, on June 25, 1953, while playing in his backyard, a bolt of spiritual lightning pierced his shoulder blades, exited his heart, ricocheted off the scorched grass and as if it had two hands wrenched his head skyward to see Christ Jesus riding on clouds, His hands cupped beneath His exposed Heart, much like is portrayed in the painting of the Scared Heart?

45 minutes later, he was holding his dying grandfather's hand who had not known anyone for the previous 3 days, spoke only of darkness and giant bugs dying of a brain tumor, but when he took hold of his grandfather's hand, his

grandfather painstakingly lifted his head slightly off his pillow, opened his eyes and whispered Pat's name, then his head fell back onto the pillow and he passed about 2 hours later.

However, his grandfather would visit him from the other side 20 years later as witnessed by Pat's fiancée and two years after that, would show up again and speak to him through a young man who resembled his grandfather, again witnessed by his now wife, and said, "If you ever need me, I'll be there for you."

To which Pat replied, "Grandad, you've spent your life here, now it's my turn; go and live in peace," never thinking that 33 years later he would call on his grandfather in desperation.

His grandfather also suffered with migraines and the gene was passed onto his mother (though she never suffered with them) through her to him and a milder case to his older brother.

One day Pat realized he had misplaced his prescribed Methadone pills and could not find them anywhere.

He called his pain management team and was told there was nothing they could do to help him until his next prescription was due (though on that call, they failed to tell him they could call in 2 prescriptions to help with his withdrawals.

It was a week later when he called in a panic they told him but said he had been through the worst of it already so might not need them. Right then and there he planned to get off both the Methadone and Percocet cold turkey and be done with so-called pain doctors.

It was determined later that both the Methadone and Percocet were creating rebound headaches, the very thing they were prescribed to alleviate if not cure).

Getting down on his knees and bawling uncontrollably, he called out to Christ and his grandfather and soon felt the most comforting peace come over him.

Robotically, he got off his knees, went into the den, grabbed the phonebook, opened it to the yellow pages to a page that had some biofeedback practitioners listed and immediately put his finger on one he had never heard of before, Quantum Biofeedback.

He called and a woman answered and told him she had a 50% off ($75.) sale for new clients, an introductory session, and he made the appointment.

During the exam after being wired up to the practitioner's computer, he was told things about himself only he knew and then was directed to the Compassion Center.

"Sounds nice but what is it?"

"It's where you get your legal medicinal marijuana card."

Having smoked and ingested marijuana in the late 60s and early 70s, he was quite aware of its effects but had no idea about using it to cure cluster migraines or anything else so he got online and researched the possible uses.

He found a medical doctor in San Diego who had written a book, bought the book, read it, and discovered the great results that doctor was having treating his cluster migraine patients with edible THC so he got his card, got some leaf from his caretaker, made some clarified marijuana butter, mixed it in a chocolate (which used to be a trigger for his migraines which he couldn't eat for over 10 years) fudge recipe.

After putting the chocolate fudge into the refrigerator to harden, he cut up the fudge into 1 inch cubes and then took a paper thin slice off a cube and put it on his tongue to melt.

He did that every morning for 9 months and suddenly one day he realized the cluster migraines were gone and did not return for over

6 years until December 2015 when new but occasional migraines invaded his mind.

But his grandad no longer responds to cries for help with his current migraines. He's now on his own since he no longer trusts any so-called pain doctors.

If a migraine episode occurs, he relies on Sumatriptan and Toradol shots which he usually gets at Urgent care. It's a little more expensive than seeing his Primary Care Physician but quicker with less hassle.

He's settled down to a pretty mundane life concentrating on serving his Maine Coon cat and enjoying his wife's company though she works fulltime being 15 years his junior.

Being retired for 15 years and staying at home fulltime except for an occasional vacation to write, he believes it's better than being committed or in jail.

Psychotherapists are out too. He doesn't believe they would keep his shared, disturbing thoughts private.

pgh nearly died when he was 3 days young. He lost half his body weight in those 3 days suffering from a staph infection he caught in the hospital.

But against all medical authorities' recommendations, his mom took him home to live or die.

She put him in a sterilized room by himself in a crib and made all his aunts and uncles (32 of them) dress in all white with masks and gloves when they came to check on him.

At 6, pgh had nightmares of characters coming at him from far away, growing in size as they approached, all dressed in white, then like balloons with the air let out, they disappeared just as they reached his bed.

pgh has also suffered over 12 concussions in his life time.

At 6 he was challenged by his older brother to leap across an attic hole but halfway through pgh thought, "I left my Superman cape at home," and fell through the hole, landing on his butt which forced his back and head backwards, slamming his head on a ladder rung, creating a spinal and cerebral concussion. He was in a coma for 3 months.

When he awoke, 2 of his elementary classmates were at his bedside and he exclaimed, "What are you doing here; you're supposed to be in school?"

pgh was also sexually molested as an 11 year old by an older male cousin which complicated his entire life even more.

He suffered 4 more concussions during 5 years of organized football starting with Pop Warner and ending in High School and wasn't allowed by college doctors to continue his football play in college without signing a legal document absolving the doctors and college of all future financial responsibility for any results of more concussions.

That was devastating to the 18 year old since his life goal was to become a football coach and his prospective college coach (who had been his high school coach at his first high school) told him if he didn't play, he would never coach which was a lie.

But pgh made the terrible decision not to play which through him into a great depression, alcoholism which caused him to lose many great jobs and marriages, and then came drugs of all kinds during years of steady unemployment with only temporary jobs here and there as he traveled the United States from West Cost to East and back, hitching across the US twice, once 2 days after Christmas from Portland Maine to Palo Alto California, making it in 74 hours and costing him and his fiancée only $4.73 since so many drivers who picked them up bought them food and drinks.

That got pgh his first newspaper job (Maine Sunday Telegram) to write a feature article on his idea to make hitchhiking a way to help drivers buy more gas during the 1973 oil crisis by having the hitchhikers buy tickets cheaply (ten cents per ticket) to give to drivers (1 ticket for every 10 miles during ride) to buy more gas since gas was being rationed.

That temporary job launched his writing career which has he was finally paid for doing. pgh has since co-authored 4 children's books with at least 1 more on the way.

Christopher Bear--Editor

Preface

At the edge of a silent river there rests a boat, its bow projecting into the muddy water; the time is unimportant, but the sky suggests the union of night and of sunshine, star shine, and dark spaces; the vessel is both worn and new; worthy of age, worthy of timelessness, and worthy of a free float upon the water; the boat moves into the water easily, but slowly, fully aware that such voyages must deal with what chance and destiny might say; it does not matter; the reeds along the shoreline bow and pipe their music in the wind, and a festival of spirit is on…

C. A. Lincoln (1972)

It does not matter
That they do not know
That I know--
I must love them
For what they do for me--
For if I do not love them
Then I know nothing,

      nothing.

Touch the Earth"*

An ancient Indian Chieftain

Sat cross-legged on a bear skin

His only separation from the earth

And he ate of the earth

Through the bear skin's pores

And the earth froze

And the bear skin froze

And the Chieftain froze

And the Chieftain thawed

And the bear skin thawed

And the earth thawed…

TITLE of poem taken from:
*Touch the Earth", T. C. McLuhan

"Birth… Copulation… Death…"

Each time I die

A new birth

The constant propagation of my soul

The hideous nine months

From verse to verse

Stamping my brain and brow

With blow to blow.

Oh, how I lie dormant

In fields of pillowy grass

Till the blades grow sharp

And puncture my soul

Allowing the blood of my verse

To flow, to flow, to strenuously flow

Into deep, dark, dry pools

Than never were.

What fiend would sip it so
With miniscule glass
      to miniscule glass
The blood that turned to wine
And criticize what I've rehearsed
And label it the vinegar
      of my soul;
I like not the sipping
      vampires of the world
Who lurk merely to quench their
        thirst
      And rob what must be told.

The man who lies down on a cross

With his head at the bottom of the cross

Needs to rest his feet

          (not a reference to Apostle Paul's death)

Man's Dilemma

While walking through a field of grass,
I picked up a slim twig
and began whipping the wind.

Hearing the wind scream in pain,
I suddenly knew why
the Flagelates
struck themselves.

But in their self inflicted pain,
they failed to realize
that they still
struck the wind.

THE WAVES OF THOUGHT

I saw her

standing on the beach,

a tall, misplaced Persian tree

taken seed in sand,

and in her bowing hand

she held a delicate peach.

I thought for a moment

that I would like to climb the tree

and the joy of boyhood danced in me

to think that I could grasp

the peach--

       so slightly out of reach.

But I have learned

the waves of thought:

Peaches fall when

ripe

without the shaking of

the bough.

No, I'll not turn

and leave her now

For there is seed

enough

in one grain of sand

to shape

a peach

in my own hand.

The meek always inherit the earth
As do great warriors,
Dead men dress alike.

The Graveyard's Calling

(dedicated to Toni Petersen)

O Mysterious Lady of the afternoon

Hastening on your late summer's journey

To the offshore distant sea.

Beware! Beware!

Of the graveyard's calling

For the dead calls to thee.

She listened to the earth's

celestial burning

And heeded not my woeful cry,

Off in an earth ship--Whirling--

Unaware--Unaware

Of the graveyard's knowing

That the Lady would not pass her by.

Over and through the monumental hills,

Headstones to the winding road,

The Lady drove and drove and drove

Searching—Ever Searching

For the great omnipotent sea,
The vastest graveyard of all.
"O Sailor--Drowned Sailor speak
strangely to me of the mysteries
contained in the undying sea
Where once poor Moses asked of thee
Divide--Divide
And let us walk free
Through the graveyard of wondrous
                    eternity,

No sailor spoke--but a woman's moan
Pierced our Lady's heart with green fire
As down from a dangling, dusty road
Silence--Icy Silence
Screamed in wonting prayer,
The shrill of the living dead.

Through the tumbled down, picket,
            graveyard gates,
Our Mysterious Lady addressed a
            massive stone,

A Mason's oration of flowery ascent
Praising—Continually Praising
The lost member of the grave woman
Who wore a white withered Rose.
"Don't sell him short,"
          the woman laughed
As if to read our Lady's thoughts,
And our Lady accepted the woman's hand
Tenderly--Lovingly
Slowly approaching the graveyard's midst,
Answering the ringing, angelus bell
          of the sea.

Two graves set side by side,
One swollen with youth
The other collapsed with age,
Adorned--Adorned
With fresh bouquets,
White Roses--headstones of the graves.

Our Lady's heart fired again
With raging desire
To grasp a bouquet and run,
Homeward--Homeward
In the distant setting sun
Before the sun plunged into the sea.

But the woman laughed
With joyous tears in her eyes
And danced around the graves as she
        cried,
"Gathering up --Gathering up"
Snips of White Roses,
Death's virginal bouquets--
        life's gift for our Lady.

Was it fair Lazarus come back from
        the dead
Clothed in womanly attire
To speak to our Lady of the smiles
After death--After death
To ease the pain
Of the birth we all desire?

"Come back again," the woman said,
And our Lady begged when?
"When you hear my cry again, dear child."
Disappearing--Disappearing
As ocean into sand,
The woman kissed our Lady's hand
        and fled.

I

SEE

THE

I

NOW

eye

sea

the

i

now

i

i

i

But my vision

is

to see

the

sea

as it

is

calm

and

ever changing.

If

i

can keep

my vision

in full

view

of

my

i

at every

now

i

will

see

the

-

no

longer

Because to sea

   the see

   is to be

      the sea

      and

      always be

      calm

      and

      ever changing.

Speech is the fool's tool

Thought is the thinker's

There are no wise men

who think and speak

Attending the Funeral
of a Friend's Father

I

Checked, Checked by worldly wind and
      residential rain
I dociled to his shuddering stanched side
The tearless passion of his pride.

My father sat beside me in the pew,
Dead gaping at the casket's waning face,
Roughing out his title's due
When he would claim his second place.

Cry, Cry, the thoughts thundered in my
      head.
Create a flood to end the torrential lull,
Your father's dead son; your father's dead,
Break the canonizing law--
      Shoot down the hovering gull.

II

I'll not face the ghastly unnatural
      social bond
That appellations have put upon
Men and Man--Father and Son
I've commuted my name to non-

Nothing is nothing;

Everything is everything;

Nothing is everything;

Everything is nothing,

But no words will ever help you

understand that

IT MATTERS NOT

It matters not
which way I go.

The crow flies west
when the sky spits snow.

But man says
he should not escape,
And the crow lies dead
in the frozen lake.

And what mourners tear
at the crow's silent wake,

Scarecrows laughing
till their bellies ache.

It matters not
which way I go,

The crow lies dead east
if she thinks she knows.
The hawk knows
the whirling chase,
And floating patience
serves to be his grace.

But there are eagles by and by
which cast another all-knowing eye.

Extinction is the way of man;

It's written everywhere
in nature's untiring plan…

Tribute to the Vietnam Police Action
(it was never an approved war)
WINDING DOWN
    Winding Down
        winding down

4 MORE DEAD
    10 More Injured
        jerrynormanduffey
the wwwaaarrr isss
           winnndinnng
              d
             o
            w
           n
            n
             n
              n
               n
                n
                 n

There are no negatives

Only positives not well received

A Child is Born

Naked,
Stashed in a crib,
I penetrated the world
Depraved,
a war disease,
Blanketed with white masked faces
and no motherly breast to feed on
but contaminated milk in abundance
from rubber nipples.

With rubber gloves
she bared me home
to immerse me in medicinal waters,
Not tears,
(for the Doctor's tears are always in vain).

Tears were forbidden.
I prospered--I mean I grew,
The depravity grew inward
invisible to Motherhood
and mother succeeded
to alter the Doctrine of the Doctor.

          Ten years I grew
like ten fingers
and ten toes
as if to prove I was normal.

Mother Victorious,
a marketplace for rubber gloves
and rubber nipples.

Ten years to witness
the trial of father and mother;
Ten years to witness
the trial of German and Jew;
Ten years without fatherly hand;
Ten years without motherly breast.

And then, like a robed cocoon,
she entered my sleepless room
for next to me a foreign baby cried
          and at Ten
I was appointed Judge of the world
and my gavel, the hall light,
pounded away at the terrycloth cocoon
and ten years of light and shadow
illuminated a wondrous, fleshy,

butterfly breast
as she bent with rubber gloves
and turned the baby over
only to return to a singular bed
of linen flesh and woolen hair.

--Ten Years--
and ten years more
to rape a hundred women,
and a hundred women reaped,
and a hundred mothers reaped,
and a thousand, chained, black-robed men
salivating.

Girl in Poetry Class

I

There she sits
Not as if she knew my glance
But as if my glance knew
Nothing but her.

Do I dare pursue?

II

My life pursues a God
Not out of habit
But out of thought,

And what if in the wake of death
God were caught?

What need of God
Would then there be?

What new God
Would then be born?

And if God be man
And man be God,
Would God then seek his own image
In beast or man?

III

Some say
"The Pursuit's The Thing"
And I add
The Pursuer--The God.

And if that rash logic
Be true,
Then I need not pursue
For we have come together
Already

At least in thought
And thought is all we have----

You need to know only what you hear

For all you hear is the truth

Nordic Lady

I've observed you
toiling in the swamps of the lower Rhine
scrubbing children's clothes.
But I've never heard you speak
Till now.

I've witnessed you
bearing the King's week's mead
across long fields of lilacs.
And angels cloud my ears with
puff balls.

I've beheld you
laboring in the fiery halls of Attila
dressing a hundred festive game birds.
And your heart is silent
and soft.

I've surveyed your
impulsive quest for fruit trees
in the wetter regions of Gaul.
And I saw your lips
move.

If someone tells you he is God,

Believe him;

If someone tells you

you are God,

Believe him;

If you believe neither of these things,

Your God is impotent

ENLIGHTENMENT

When you know
you know
and the very minute
you want to
tell
someone
you know
is the very minute
that you
must become
silent
and
let someone
else
tell everyone
you know

This is how enlightenment
is attained;

Those people with the
wisdom
and
patience
to share that
wisdom
with those who need
it
at a precise moment
are
enlightened.

Then you
as an enlightened being
must sit
and
watch
everyone else
struggle along their
path
to find their own
enlightenment,
and for you to

remain

enlightened

you

must

remain

silent

and

reassuring.

Alternative

(rebuttal to "Rage, rage against the dying of the light")

If I had my choice of death--
One capsule, one gasp of breath.

But death looms like poisonous gas
Seeps thought doors without a rasp
And chokes its victim with surprise
As the victim struggles, fights, yet
   dies.

So I shall not try to cheat death's goal,
I'll wait and wait as I grow old--
Then when death is strychnine strong
I'll turn and smile and shout,
    "COME ON!"

If you seek the truth,
Listen, it is all you hear;
There is only one absolute truth,
Love;
All other truths are merely
Expressions of love
Clothed in traveler's garments

The Path of a Madman

I

Here we are
Wandering around aimlessly,
Waiting for that <u>warning</u> bell
   to ring
    that silent scream
    that says somewhere
     someone
     needs help!

And in our path
   stand all the
books, laws, visions,
inventions, and contraptions
   of every other
    man
that are supposed to help us
   help that one
     person
   who is screaming
    for help
   but by their very creation
they prevent us from ever helping.

II

Now suppose
It is winter,
and I were to tell
someone right now
that I was walking
through the cold of winter
Naked--
(I didn't start out that way
mind you,
I was fully clothed
but the path was that long
that now I am naked)

and I was searching
to find and help that
one person
who is still crying on the cross.

--They'd put me away--

A flower asks not for rain and sunshine

But receives them all the same

Compromise

Let me not forget
the quiet year I consumed
miracle making in her bed,

the tedious theft of time,
the way the incessant clock ticks

                                              away

unnoticed
but by punctual sun and moon,

Death's sheets washed live
with colored lime,
the grave made fresh again
to admit the kill another day.

Do not let me forget
how I murdered myself
on that bloodied white-gown day.

A Lover Lost

I will not compare you to the songs
   of nature's way,
For you are not as lovely as a rose
   in full bloom
Nor air the beauteous scents of a
   Summer's day
(Where they abound in shades of
   Winter's doom).
Ah, but as a jewel among jewels how
   rare you'd be,
Such brilliance only mans' craft
   bestows upon nature's throne,
Or as a thief among thieves who'd out
   steal their thievery,
Nature would steal you away to leave me
   quite alone.
Such thoughts possess me and in my
   shameless, selfish pride;
I grant you immortality for nature grant
   you naught.
Thus, in my memory you remain a chaste
   and lustful bride
But in nature only a mortal stripped of
   your gown to rot.
Therefore, I cherish you though I be
   in my Winter's seat
Where fires roar in search of long
   lost Summer's heat.

Portrait of Still Life

Silent dolls

Lie on hard beds

Concentrating on blank ceilings.

Show no pain,

Shed no tears,

Who hears their cry

To live--

To die--

The electric light bulb
      was invented out of
          Love
      to save all energies
      from darting around
          and colliding
      with each other
          in the dark
          in search of
Light

Zen Exercise 3223

sit

and

think

somewhere there

is

someone

in danger

and

someone else

helping them

You pick up the phone

and

call them

and

suddenly

they say

"I'll call you back"

and you now know

that anything you do

exceptsit

and

wait

and

think

is to prevent

them

from helping the best

they can

and

then have someone

come in the room

and

say

"I've got to use the phone"

and

let them.

The rich and the poor

Know the TRUTH,

Everyone else is still seeking

There once was a young man
        who searched for pain
and therefore never felt the rain
but wallowed in the sunshine
        whenever it came.

His search for pain
was so treacherous it's said
that he took a rock to his head;
his head did bleed, his nose did snort
and soon he was off to bed

While in bed
        a Magician came
to warn him of his search for pain,
"why not seek a life of joy instead?"
the Magician said with slight disdain

"I will, I will," the boy exclaimed
"But won't it be as just insane?"

i took out the answering service.
No one ever calls.
Yet the white virginal phone
hangs on the wall.

Games People Play

wolf,

    ha,

        woolf,

            ha, ha,

            Wooolf,

                Ha, Ha, Ha,

WOOOOOOOOOOOOOOOOOOOLF,

    HAHAHAHAHAHAHAHAHA!!!!!!!

DEATH!

The answer to life's hidden secret

May be found by picking up

A piece of dry ice

Psychiatry
may do well
to listen to
a client's
extension of themselves
to help the
clients
help those
who
are their extensions.

if the client's
extension
is only one
person,
then the client
need only
help
himself
to
become
whole
and therefore
need no further
help
other than to
take up
Psychiatry

Who Goes to the Calling Place?

A thousand more come
and forbid me to walk
as my glorious Father ambulated,
and a thousand more come
and forbid me His touch of Summer
      trees,
and I become the only paw-paw
and a thousand more come
and forbid me His breath of air,
and I become the silent wind of
      Winter
and a thousand more come
and forbid me His taste of water's
      wine,
and I become a lonely drop of grape
      in a tarnished cup
and a thousand more come
and burn the ruffled Autumn pages
      of His unseasonal book

and I become but a leaf
that spins in silent winds
that swirls in calm waters
that falls from living branches
and dies when engulfed in iron-
        gated gutters

        Let not the man-made gutters
                be the calling place
                of dying leaves
                be the calling place
                for all Mankind.

A Beachcomber's Love

It's late,
The night air is warm--
the sea whispers gently
to the shore
then retracts its caress
like an anxious lover
who's too often loved.

afar,
the single drone of a foghorn
beckons to a wandering vessel
like the outstretched fingers
of a woman's hand
pressed lightly
on her lover's thigh;

too soon
the raging sun
dashes after
the cool moon as i stand blushing
caught in the midst of God's endless affair...

The Stage Was Set
(Saturday afternoon matinee circa 1950)

The stage was set;
Hundreds of children flocked
to see the show.

It was a different age.

On the screen,
A long-haired bearded man
dressed in a white flowing robe
walked from person to person
touching them.

As I sat in the audience
watching,
waiting
for my time to come,

The serial ended abruptly.

Another man,
A living man,
dressed in a tightly fitted suit
wheeled a large fish bowl
onto the stage,

(fish replaced by hundreds
of muddled pennies
and one brilliant silver dime)

Clutched in my hand,
an orange ticket,
a stub
with an absurd progression
of numbers stamped on its face.

The man spun a cylindrical barrel,
picked out an orange ticket
and called out a number,
not mine.

The man called out another,
not mine.

The man called out,
not mine by one digit

Absurd!

In a flash,
the boy next to me
grabbed my ticket
and replaced it with his.

Before I knew
what had transpired,
I was on stage.

Fifth in line

Absurd!

The first boy tried for the dime,
missed,
twenty-five dirty pennies to the good,
grief for the missing dime.

The second boy,
the same--less two cents

The third,
no dime

The fourth,
no dime

The fifth--
my trembling fingers
surrounded by passed over pennies
felt for the rough edge of the one
brilliant
silver dime.

I cheated;
I won;
Victory was mine.

Treasures:
 Tickets to future serials,
 Candy--Pop Corn--
 Noise Makers.

Five more sad boys in line,

And one exuberant boy in the audience
                    Crying out--Crying out,
          "It was my ticket stub.
          It was my winning ticket stub!"

And half the spoils became his

And all the glory was mine.

SELF-KNOWLEDGE

We are the aged
forbidden to pass among the young?

we are the deceivers
caged in by the righteous;
we are the insane
walled in by the sane.

You, You are the young,
        the righteous,
        the sane,

If by some quirk
you must enter our colony,
we will accept you,

For we are the aged,
we are the deceivers,
we are the insane
and know full well
who we are

If you have to ask for anything
You don't need it
For you will always receive
only what you need
From those who know what you need.

I thirst to sip
the sweet milk
of a woman's breast
But I cannot bear
the thought
that a child may need it more than I.

To give life
is to give life
Nothing more;

To take life
is to take life
Nothing less,

and it is so
damn necessary
to live

If you read a lot,

you haven't found the answer;

If you write a lot,

you haven't found the answer;

If you listen a lot,

You will help everyone

find the answer

Mount Evans, Colorado

There must have been a time,

in man's time,

when no man set foot here,

when God walked this land

unafraid of crushing humans

with his soft silent steps.

But concrete roads have changed this mount

or was it the first man

who chased God to this summit

and caught glimpse of Him

and out of love returned with more men.

How love multiplies in strange ways

My foot too has now overturned a stone

cheating the snow's work

and trampled on some wild flower

destroying the food of some silent creature.

Look, there's an eagle in flight
        from his nest.
Would I be food enough for him
        with Winter coming on yet?

I have gladly

wept

at the beauty

of delicately carved marble statues,

But the weeping

was external

and the Greeks

cry with me

to know

the Art

is never the real

thing.

Now,

there is a statuesque

Madonna

who roams

my soul

and opens

a thousand doors

that Hesse would

be ashamed

to know,

and

a million

tiny tear drop

bombs

explode

unceasingly

and crevasse

my mind,

and the City of Atlantis

was consumed by

tears

and Yosemite has twice been

swallowed by the

sea

and California will feed the

ocean,

and my mind's evolution

ends

and

begins

with you.

Zero Population Growth

It's okay
to have children
and as many as you
think
is necessary
to have
as long as you
can always
give
your children
exactly what they need
at every moment of
your
life.

If you can't do
it
for one child,
become you won
child

and mother

him

or

her

so tenderly

and

pamperingly

that you will

mother

all the earth's

children

if that is

who

your

child

or

mother

is.

If

i

tell you something

and

you find it

to

be

truth

then i know

the

truth.

But if i

tell

you

something

and

you know

it

isn't

truth--

P

F

C

R

If you meet someone on a sunlit street
Say hello and know everything is okay.

If you meet someone in a dark alley,
Strike a match, say hello, and know
		everything is okay.

If you see someone drowning in the ocean,
Don't strike a match or say hello,
But jump in to save yourself
And you both will live together in
		eternity,
As you did on the sunlit street and
		in the dark alley.

Carmen, The Black Rose

Would we had months enough
I'd played at the nape of your neck
Like a child treasures his sand box,
Grain by grain, kissing the sand away

Would we had years enough
I'd taken you body in mouth around the
world
And stamped the fare coins with love
And pots of gold would lie at your
fingertips

Would we had centuries enough
I'd carried you through the tomb
of Romeo and Juliet
To share the secrets of their youth
And pass among the Garden of our Birth

But time is the crook in crime
And minutes but all we have
To sip black rose petal wine
And devour the fire white meat of lust

The man who plays chess to win,
Loses;
The man who plays chess to lose,
Wins;
Two men who play chess together to lose
Draw and win each other.

Two Strangers in Salt Lake City

You aged men,

You know who dwells here,

The song of the fur-feathered wren

Needs your tending ears.

Do the signs of age

Grow so receding on my brow

To let us share the equipage

Of now and now and forever now?

I'll not disappoint you

For I too am in touch with time

Though for you and you and you

Who knows not the forest's rhyme,

Let's talk of men and trees alone,

Such stuff that makes a thorny throne.

If a writer gets published,

It is not because he has something to say

But because he could type well

We All Succeed

RUN

    RUN

        FOOLS of the EARTH

To catch

    a BUS

        to NOWHERE,

and nowhere comes soon enough
to steal the failures from all men
and grant them their success
in the HOUR of NOTHINGNESS.

If someone says he'll bring you pleasure,

become Pavlov's dog

and you will receive pleasure

Liberation

How long have I worn the pants

Not to know of what gender I am

Nor to care for ecstatic bowel movements

That flush to gutters to smell up the

world--

Men are Men.

Women are Women.

Men are Women.

Women are Men.

So sings the fur-feathered wren.

Man's Evolutionary Progress

"Look at the dead trees in the orchard,
father. Why are they dead?"
"They're dormant, son."
"But why are the dead, father?"
"It's winter, son."
"Will they ever come back to life?"
"In the spring, I guess."

"Look, father, there's a big steel crane."
"What's it doing, son?"
"The crane's pulling out the dead trees,
father.
I thought you said they'd come back to life
in the spring?"
"Yes, son, but next spring there'll be tall buildings
to replace the trees."

"Will the buildings die in Winter, father?"

Bearded men,
bell-bottom, trousered ladies
fish for words
from the pond of sweet scented air,

and their catch is like mine,
and their words are much the same,
and our worlds--though dressed differently--
are economically sound
and too damn tame.

Gravestones are epitaphs of stupidity;

The earth accepts the new born geniuses

Without them

Winter Walking

It's cold.
The snow is like
wet, heavy pillow-feathers.

It's colder now.
i'm on my knees,
        but i've been there before.

It's not unbearable, not yet.
If it gets too cold
Death's blanket will bring me
                warmth,

or the Sun
        may soon appear
and cheat death's gift
                another day.

Buddha said
"Don't just do something,
Stand there"

When a
worker bee
invades your path
in full flight,
wings buzzing
like cannons,
or bassoons,
become the
flower
that you are
and deny him
his
pollen
but grant him
his life's only purpose

and the worker bee
will cease to be
a threat to you

so buzz off, man

Home for Christmas

Blood reigns
like a monsoon--
and I sit in my freezing room
sweating profusely--
Afraid of the jungle
Outside,
Afraid of the jungle
Within me--

Where to turn?
to a foxhole?
to a cot?
to a bed of straw
yellow with hue,
damp with perspiration?

Yet, my blood runs hot
within me--

Only a trace of myself
left, like a hidden fossil
imprinted forever
in the ground.

who to turn to
but to God....

A Measure of Time

Where does time go?

i can measure it by the
candles i light each night.

Six candles--three nights gone.

You'd think the wax
would just melt down
and cover the candle holder
so you could build it up again
and make another candle

But it doesn't.

It just disappears somewhere
and it doesn't do any good to
wonder where.

i guess i'll start keeping track
by the number of empty wine bottles
that the garbage man picks up from
my door each morning.

Six empty wine bottles--two nights gone.

Poetry is just a word;

Poems are just groups of words;

Poetic license is the tool used to say

Nothing,

And be understood.

Therefore, everyone is a poet

A Madman's Vision

I

Alone
I struggled for the door,
the front door,
the only door out.

The hall's white washed walls
created an impenetrable maze
and left me banging my head
waiting for the bell to ring.

Where was the Doctor?
The Researcher?
The Great Experimenter?

Uncontrolled, I crawled back
to my room and flung myself
on the bed and clung, clung
with the claws of a Madman.

There was no spinning of the room
except the spinning of all rooms
shared by all madmen.

My head was not soaked in cocaine
nor embroiled by acidic delusions.

I have no excuses.

Mad--Hah Hah--I was at once, Mad.

Round and round Mount Rushmore goes
Where is stops only madmen know;
          Hi George--Hi Tom--Hi Ted
               Howdy Abe,
and the stiffly carved stone faces
               become one
the mask of all Mankind
               Dramatis Personae,
and the silent wind blew the bones
          out of the stone hills.

And then there was light,
extreme bright light,
not the light
of a million burning candles,
nor the light of dawning,
Not the first light,
not the light that any Madman
had seen before,
But the total absence of blackness.

White washed air
penetrated by three vague women,

Macbeth! Macbeth!

No, not the witches of Macbeth;
They were never so alive.

Long purple flowing robes
encased blank, non-apparent
Faces;

What happened to the faces?
What happened to the masks?

II

I knew of a young boy once,
Cancer stole his face
in the hands of a tender nurse's
Care.

III

Nurses--were they my tending nurses?

Gone--Come back!
Tell me who you are!

104

Why weren't you mermaids singing?
A clue--A clue,
God I must have a clue!

Blackness,
Not darkness,
not the darkness of a solemn wintry night
but the total absence of whiteness.
Was this to be my only clue?

No stars,
no guiding stars
where managers lurk--where managers lurk
to be found by wise men only.

A Madman's Night--but it was not night,
just Mid-afternoon.

Where was the true vision?

All madmen have visions
and talk to themselves
of the vision--the only vision--

There was neither fire nor ice!

IV

Once, as a child,
playing in my backyard
on a dismal, foggy day—a grey day

I had a vision,
A flash of light,
Not the light of the first light,

My God--The Son of God!
Where? In the sky!

Who are you talking to?

Who would listen but a Madman?
myself, of course!

Can you substantiate the vision?
"Pilot Blinded By Extreme Light"

V

It rained soon after
on that grey, dismal day,

Cancelled the long awaited family picnic.

There was a phone call

My Grandpa lay dying in his spinning
                Madman's bed
talking of bugs--of blackness--of
                giant bugs.

The Intern said
"A simple diagnosis--
A brain tumor
was killing him"
(and his vision)

Grandpa and his wife had eleven children
Two passed on when very young
Nine lived to bear more children;

All gathered around his bed,

Children,
Grandchildren,
Great Grandchildren,

His wife,

And a young Madman.

Grandpa know no one,
not even his wife;

His outstretched hand
grasped for someone;

I was nearest and took his hand
In full voice he cried out my name
and died.

A Madman's Vision?

Maybe?

VI

A Madman's Void:
Darkness--the total absence of whiteness,
Then blackness penetrated by whiteness.

A man?
A vision of a man?
He was no ordinary city dweller
clothed in total whiteness
walking alone--alone
in a blackened void.

Don't ask me how many steps he took;
Madmen can't keep count!

From behind the man,
from out of the void,
into a Madman's reality
flew a pure, soft, white dove
and speeded the man on his way
back into the void
from where he came.

The nowhere,
where Madmen
 go now and then

A vision?

No--just a mid-afternoon dream--
Visions are only for Madmen----

Blessed be the misunderstood;

Blessed be Christ;

Blessed be the Devil;

Blessed be the Silent.

Be sure to pray for Christ's return!